EMERGENCE

Volume 1 - Introduction

by Rosemary Wilkie

Text copyright © 2013/2019 Rosemary Wilkie

All rights reserved

Published by Morgan Books

For my teachers
Dr Don Beck
Christopher Cooke

ACKNOWLEDGEMENTS

Anne Verity for her wisdom and unfailing
support

Janet Derwent who commissioned for
The Sundial House Group members and students
the original six articles
on which this book is based

Cover design by Paul Effenberg of Vine Designs

ALSO BY ROSEMARY WILKIE

*French translation of Emergence Vol 1 –
Introduction*

Children's books:

Emily and the Angels
Tom and Who?
Poppy's Quest

PREFACE

Everyone is doing the best they can, all the time. Yes, really! Even if what they do looks stupid or wrong to observers - anger, violence, blaming others, running away, not doing what they agreed to, taking refuge in illness - may be the only way a person can cope. The only way they know *how* to cope at their stage of development.

Spiral Dynamics Integral (SDi) theory shows that human nature changes as the conditions of life change. And that we have the in-built capacity to develop more complex thinking to handle new problems in new life conditions. We observe this evolution in children as they grow, but it also applies to adults and even to whole societies.

So if you have ever wondered why people think the way they do, why some are so difficult to deal with, why they disagree with each other so much, this book is for you.

Please note: this book is a straight reprint of the Kindle version published in 2012.
Volume 2 will be published in 2019.

We wake and find ourselves on a stair; there are stairs below us which we seem to have ascended, there are stairs above us which go out of sight.

Ralph Waldo Emerson

TABLE OF CONTENTS

CHAPTER 1 - INTRODUCTION

The law of evolution governs life on earth.
No form of life can remain unchanged for long without
crystallising and disappearing.
Michal Eastcott.

Turmoil in the world's financial markets since 2008 is a striking lesson about the global interdependence of the human race. It burst upon us when we were already deeply concerned about climate change, food and water supply, social deprivation, and the terrorism and wars arising endlessly between peoples with conflicting ideals and belief systems.

Economists and politicians are trying to recapture pre-2008, and failing. We can't go back. We are being forced to question everything we took for granted and at the same time expand our awareness to the entire world.

Fourteen billion years ago an awesomely powerful impulse sprang from the void, creating energy, light, matter, galaxies, stars and planets, Earth, the mineral, vegetable and animal kingdoms. And, more recently, as life became more complex and organised, it produced consciousness.

We still don't really know how we, homo sapiens, came to be, or why. So we let the experts argue about it and focus on the material world, forgetting the wholeness of the patterns of life in which we are involved. Throughout the ages the life force has fought for its very existence, but its germ of intention, its will to continually evolve, has never wavered.

History records many examples of turbulence, profound change and mass migrations. With hindsight we see that it is during chaotic times that great new ideas appear. We urgently need new ideas, because as Einstein said, no problem can be solved from the level of consciousness that created it. Tribal antipathy, that would once have had only local significance, can now have world-wide implications. It is no longer possible to ignore growing separation between the haves and the have-nots in the world, or to deny the impact of our life-style and technological advances on the planet. Humpty Dumpty has fallen off the wall and all the king's horses and men (i.e. our total resources) cannot put him back together again.

The Ageless Wisdom and modern research now combine in what is known as developmental psychology, defining distinct stages of development that swing from the individual to the collective and back. Maslow's hierarchy of needs is well known. Robert Kegan, Jean Piaget and Jane Loevinger produced other classifications.

However the most significant contribution to the field is not a classification or a typology at all, it is a comprehensive view of change. Clare W. Graves, a professor of psychology in Union College, New York, applied developmental psychology to groups and societies. He studied *values*, asking each interviewee to describe how their ideal person would behave in certain situations or life conditions. A clear pattern emerged, a pattern validated by subsequent research and experience.

His painstaking research, begun in 1952, showed how the sequentially emerging stages are themselves organised within a larger dynamic system, and are related to each other within a living evolutionary spiral of development. Each stage is shaped by its relationship to the other stages. Every baby as it grows recapitulates human cultural history. Psychology is a *process.*

After Graves died in 1986, his work was continued by Dr Don Beck and his research assistant Christopher Cowan. In their book *Spiral Dynamics,* published in 1996, they ascribed colours to the stages of development for easier comprehension:

BEIGE: Acts instinctively to survive, like a new born baby or tsunami victim.

PURPLE: In fearful primitive times, we thought frightening natural forces were powerful gods, and placated them with rituals and sacrifice.

RED: When these rituals began to stifle us, some began to think 'what about me?' and asserted themselves ruthlessly, craving honour and heroism.

BLUE: In the ensuing anarchy and chaos, we sought order and meaning, and found it in self-sacrificing and unquestioning obedience to an absolute God or king.

ORANGE: When individuals found absolute order oppressive and became tired of waiting for future reward, they competed to create the good life for themselves here and now.

GREEN: When materialism failed to bring happiness, we became egalitarian and turned inwards to rediscover a social conscience and spirituality.

Each stage represented *new thinking for new times*, transcending and including what had gone before.

Each stage is called a vMeme, building on Richard Dawkins' use of 'meme' to describe units of cultural information: e.g. Puritan work ethic, power dressing. A vMeme – a values Meme - is like a container in which our values and beliefs form and fit, and which attracts and repels others. Our core values and beliefs are tucked away so deeply inside of us that we are not usually aware of them, and are surprised when others do not share them.

In the First Tier stages above, conflict arises because people cannot understand the thinking of those with a different centre of gravity.

For example: the peasant clearing a patch of rain forest thinks of feeding his family, the buyer of his cows will fight to keep his job, the corporation that employs him thinks of its profits, westerners campaigning to preserve the rainforest worry about global warming and the future of the planet. Different life conditions. Different ways of thinking.

It is only when we make the momentous leap into Second Tier, which begins with **YELLOW** and **TURQUOISE**, that we gain the ability to see and appreciate the whole spiral, which enables us to understand all the First Tier stages. It is estimated that 10% of the world population have stabilised in a Second Tier way of thinking, and between 10-15% are exiting **Green** with the potential to move to Second Tier.

As we moved from **Blue** to **Orange** we began to think differently and put our trust in science. Science has provided us with innumerable benefits, but has itself become a belief system. Too many of us shrug and say, 'Science and technology will provide the answers to global problems.'

No doubt they will contribute enormously, but the global population is growing faster than our resources. So we must outgrow the confines of an exclusive belief in science and integrate it with spirituality so that the two co-exist and are no longer regarded as mutually exclusive. This is necessary to support the continual development of both. We have evolved in a similar way many times before.

Spiral Dynamics Integral will enable you to see yourself and those around you with greater clarity and compassion, and gain profound insight into the challenges of life in the twenty-first century.

Evolution is at work, and our individual and collective decisions are already shaping the future. We are co-creators of evolution. The responsibility is ours.

CHAPTER 2 - THE vMEMES

Below you will find descriptions of the vMemes at their peak or most intense. The distinct entering and leaving phases will be described in Volume 2.

As we are born and grow, we gradually build a personal 'meme stack'. Starting with Beige in babyhood, we add levels of consciousness in the order described below. We don't lose the earlier levels - we transcend and include them. We can, and do, call on them in different areas of our lives. Perhaps Orange at work, Green for voluntary work and Red for sport.

THE FIRST TIER comprises six vMemes.

The first level of human existence is **BEIGE.**
Do what you must to stay alive. The level of primitive man, an intelligent animal with finely developed instincts that have atrophied in us. We need food, water, shelter, warmth. Think of a new baby, street people, refugees, the elderly with Alzheimer's. We can all regress temporarily to Beige when faced with catastrophe or illness.

As survival needs are met, new brain connections form. We shift into emotional **PURPLE** and form tribal groupings for safety. Blood bonds are strong. We obey the chieftain and share food. We make gods of the forces of nature over which we have no control - and the shaman intervenes for us. We preserve sacred spaces and rituals appease our ancestral spirits to stay

safe. Storytellers keep inherited wisdom alive. This is
the world of indigenous people, such as the Aborigines
of Australia and the Maori of New Zealand, who have a
sensitivity to the natural world and other talents that we
have lost.

On a personal level Purple is the end of infancy when
the magic word 'Mama' brings what you need. Scream
if she disappears, don't walk on the cracks and never
go to bed without your teddy bear. Parental bonding is
crucial to the healthy development and self esteem of
children. (10% of world population, 1% of power).

Once we feel safe and secure, we can become
conscious of ourselves as separate individuals, and
start to feel angry. We question our leaders and seek
personal autonomy. The strongest battle for the top
places. Audacious spirits challenge the gods. Losers
are expelled from the herd. We are into RED. And the
terrible twos! Instant gratification, no sense of guilt, no
thought of consequences. We grab what makes us feel
good without regard for others. Anything that goes
wrong must be somebody else's fault. If we are
thwarted our rage is excessive, our reactions violent.
We demand respect and our greatest fear is losing
face, being shamed.

This world is full of aggression, selfishness, hostility and
battles for power. It is the world of slavery, feudalism,
heroes and conquest, Genghis Khan, James Bond
villains, mercenaries, rock stars, sports teams, sales
teams and street gangs in deprived inner cities.

Those living at this level do so because that is what their life conditions demand. However Red is also extremely creative. It gives us courage and the strength to defend ourselves. It gets things done, inspires heroic acts, breaks with limiting traditions and opens up new pathways. (20% of world population and 5% of power)

The move to **BLUE** occurs when we become desperate to find order and a purpose in life to explain all our suffering. The movement may be political, cultural, religious or nationalistic. It lays down absolute rules and laws, discipline is strict but fair and often public. Blue allots places for everyone in its hierarchy, and makes those who don't conform feel guilty. We are expected to sacrifice for the common good. There is only one right way to think and the virtuous are rewarded (in this life or the next).

This vMeme supports industrial economies: Taiwan, Malaysia, Mexico. It is the world of guides and scouts, the Salvation Army, Confucian China, Puritan America, Hassidic Judaism and Islamic fundamentalism. As such belief systems clash, Blue can be the most warlike of the vMemes.

But it can also be the most peaceful. When you start school, you learn about fair and unfair, right and wrong, and what happens when you disobey. Other people have rights and sometimes it pays to wait for what you want. Our society now would not function well without the infrastructure of laws and institutions created by peaceful healthy Blue, as it controls the chaos of Red. (40% of world population and 30% of power)

Eventually some people start to criticise authority, question the rules, find new and better ways of doing things, or simply rebel against the constraints. The Arab Spring was a good example. 'What about me?' they cry, echoing Red rebelling against Purple.

ORANGE appeared in the 18th century, and is now the predominant vMeme in our western society. Achievement, competitiveness, technology and the good life. Success is highly rewarded. The new brain connections we have developed enable us to be rational, keep track of multiple interests and shift attention between them. We are mobile, pragmatic, opportunistic, independent and in control of most areas of our lives. We stand or fall by our own efforts and talents. When we are no longer useful, we are scrapped like obsolete technology. Orange usually results in a free market economy and multi-party democracy. (30% of world population and 50% of power)

After a while we see the downside of Orange, the numbers of have-nots, the disastrous effect of 'progress' on our planet. We see that material success and possessions do not create happiness and begin to adjust our priorities. There has to be more to life! We have begun to think in a new way and develop a social conscience. And so we come to the top of the first tier of vMemes: **GREEN**, which began to spread in the mid 19th century.

We cultivate our inner child and seek a purpose in life. We try to bring peace to society by resolving inequalities. We realise that individual actions do matter. This is the world of GreenPeace, Amnesty International, academia, public education, anti-discrimination legislation, political correctness and animal rights.

Egalitarian and humanitarian, we campaign for the rain forests and against GM foods, feel guilty about things our country has done in the past and make amends, boycott multinationals who abuse third world employees, buy Free Trade goods, grow organic food, join groups and accept their thinking to make ourselves acceptable, make decisions (eventually) by consensus when everyone has had their say, share ideas and feelings, meditate for peace, believe in the importance of all living things, create caring communities and enthuse about the wonderful new age we are creating.

However caring for everyone and everything, for example in health care, can be overwhelming, emotionally and financially. We can be very judgmental about those who do not share our ideas, and see those in other vMemes through our own Green filter. For example, seeing brutal young criminals as simply deprived youths.

Group pressures can be extreme and those of us who do not accept the group's norms – even including what it is right to wear - are criticised, made to feel guilty or even excluded. We begin to feel stifled by the collective, reassert our individuality and do what needs to be done by ourselves instead of waiting until everyone is happy about it. (10% of world population and 15% of power)

When the centre of gravity of our consciousness is locked in to First Tier thinking, it is nearly impossible to understand the thinking of any of the others, however hard we try. If there are people in our lives we can never agree with, their consciousness is probably centred in a different vMeme.

For example, **Red** thinks **Blue** is repressive. **Blue** thinks **Orange** is pushy. **Orange** thinks **Green** is barmy. Many **Greens** who believe themselves highly spiritual are in fact regressing to the pre-rational comfort of **Purple**. **Green**, thinking it has all the answers, scorns **Orange** that produces the wealth that **Green** generously wants to share out. **Green** cannot see that the drive and expertise of **Orange** can be harnessed to resolve the problems that **Green** has identified.

THE SECOND TIER

The shift to Second Tier **YELLOW** is momentous (and only a small but growing percentage of the world population has made it so far). Yellow began after WWI, spurred on by the beat generation of the 1950s. Our ability to cope with complexity becomes greater than the sum of all the earlier six stages put together.

We no longer perceive the world only from the human angle. We now see it from a universal perspective - a radically different viewpoint. We live fully, tread lightly on the earth, treasure the wonders of life above material possessions, rate knowledge and competence above power and status, cooperate, do more in less time. We can see the whole picture, how each vMeme builds on the preceding one and how everything fits together in one enormous never-ending spiral of life. We can at last begin to see what each individual, organisation or country needs to help it evolve to the next level and what each contributes to the spiral.

We engage in personal and spiritual development, become skilled in conflict resolution and cultivate a spirit of reconciliation.

Beyond Yellow is TURQUOISE, which appeared in the 1960s and is about global synthesis and renewal, recognising that we are both individuals and part of a larger compassionate whole. According to Dr. Graves, this Second Tier also consists of six levels of complexity and CORAL is just beginning to appear. Our brains cannot yet begin to comprehend the Second Tier stages beyond that, or the far distant Third Tier.

DO YOU RECOGNISE YOURSELF AND OTHERS?

BEIGE

This is where we all began as babies and where we may end our lives, living instinctually from day to day, relying on others for safety, water, food, and warmth.

PURPLE

Toddlers and tribes-people form strong bonds with family or tribe, sharing everything with them and opposing outsiders. We believe our storytellers' myths of origin and confuse them with facts. We are superstitious, observe rituals, see 'signs' in events, and carry tokens for luck. We tread lightly on the earth.

RED

'I'm the king of the castle, get down you dirty rascal!'
Tough leaders emerge and attract followers. We
demand respect and impose our will without guilt,
careless of consequences - which are never our fault! If
crossed, we have to get even. Our only fear is being
shamed. But we are also imaginative, creative,
energised, fun loving and free.

BLUE

The child learns right from wrong. Order replaces
anarchy. Everyone has their place in a hierarchy. Our
lives acquire meaning from a truth, a cause or righteous
pathway, and non-believers deserve punishment. We
obey authority, apply rules and regulations, and delay
satisfying personal urges in exchange for future reward
- on earth or in heaven. We are learning guilt based
self-discipline.

ORANGE

'I did it my way.' We embrace technology and change to
acquire the good life and material abundance, letting go
of tradition and following fashion. We compete and play
to win, and believe that optimistic, risk-taking and self-
reliant people deserve success, and that the earth's
resources are there for us to help ourselves. We often
abandon those who can't keep up.

GREEN

We seek peace with our inner Self, and explore with others the caring dimensions of community. We long to free humanity from greed, dogma and separativeness, and spread the earth's resources equally among everyone. We reach decisions through reconciliation and consensus, and it may be difficult for the individual to disagree.

YELLOW

Fear has dropped away. We are inner directed, live fully and responsibly, and act according to the needs of the situation. We see that all levels of the spiral are essential for its viability, and can understand the thinking of people living in those life conditions. We value the magnificence of existence over material possessions, and don't waste time on trivia.

TURQUOISE

We stand in awe of the cosmic order and its creative forces. We believe that our Self is both distinct and part of this larger, conscious, spiritual whole in which everything is connected to everything else. We see the big picture, think holistically, intuitively and expansively, and cooperate for the greater good of all species.

CHAPTER 3 – BASIC PRINCIPLES

*There is no finality in the presentation of truth; It develops
and grows to meet man's growing demand for light.*
Michal J. Eastcott

History is full of turbulence, the migration of peoples
and other profound changes which occasionally erupt
into epochal change such as the agricultural and
industrial revolutions. We are now experiencing not only
rapid technological advances, but a revolution in
consciousness to which SDi is a precious guide, a
silken thread to hold on to as we navigate our way
through the maze of chaos, uncertainty, hope and fear.

Why a spiral? Its elegant form connects everything to
everything else. It is universal, found everywhere from
the double helix of the DNA molecule and tiny seashells
to giant distant galaxies. SDi is about the forces inside
human spirals that coil through individual minds, lift
organisations to new levels and drive First Tier societies
to evolve.

In Chapter 2 we looked at the peak expression of the
vMemes. Movement within and between vMemes is
complex and will be covered in Volume 2. But first we
must understand the core principles.

1 Human nature is not fixed.
Professor Graves said, 'Human nature is a *process*
marked by the progressive subordination of older
behavioural systems to newer, higher order systems.' In
other words, we have the capacity to upgrade or re-

calibrate ourselves in response to changing life conditions, without losing touch with the older ways of being. Indeed we may be at different levels in our work, family or personal life.

2 vMemes are a product of the interaction of our intelligence systems with our life conditions.
Life conditions have four main aspects:
- <u>Times:</u> Change is faster in some places, slower in others.
- <u>Place</u>: Physical conditions, natural and man-made.
- <u>Problems:</u> Needs and fears of the group.
- <u>Circumstances:</u> Social role, educational level, gender, race, appearance, inner life.

When these life conditions change through war, economics or from natural causes, vMemes may emerge, surge, regress or fade in response. When a new level is activated, we have the potential to think out ways to change our behaviour patterns and rules for living to adapt to the new conditions.

3 vMemes zig-zag between expressive and self-sacrificing themes.
The warm colours **BEIGE RED ORANGE** and **YELLOW** represent self-expression, focusing on the outside world in order to master or change it. In the First Tier, self-expressive systems thrive in hierarchy.
Beige expresses itself to survive and reproduce itself
Red expresses itself at all costs
Orange expresses itself confidently and logically
Yellow expresses itself by being true to itself, but never at the expense of others.

The cool colours **PURPLE** **BLUE** **GREEN** and
TURQUOISE are sacrificial, surrendering self-interest
for the good of the communal/collective whole
Purple sacrifices itself for the protocol of the tribe
Blue sacrifices itself for reward in this life or the next
Green sacrifices itself to be accepted by the group.

These are the primary swings between:
- I/We; autonomy/position in group; reliance on external
input, and
- Trusting our internal judgment; exploring and
mastering the outer world by achieving peace with our
inner world.

**4 vMemes emerge along the Spiral in a wave-like
fashion**.
vMemes may seem to appear suddenly, but they come
in like a wave on the beach, overlapping the receding
wave of the previous system. They have an entering
phase of preparation and excitement, then a peak
phase of apparent stability (which we saw in Chapter
2), and an exiting period of disintegration as problems
outstrip the capacity to deal with them.

During a period such as we are experiencing now, the
mass of people and the media focus on what is
apparently going wrong, while the new era grows
strongly, drawing on untapped potential - mostly
unseen, though sometimes attacked by the previous
system - while it prepares to 'suddenly' burst on to the
scene. Rather like a singer or writer who has an
'overnight success' for which they have worked
unnoticed for twenty years.

5 Each new vMeme builds on the foundation of those which went before, adding new levels of complexity of thinking, more diversity of organisational forms, more alternative ways of doing things, and more freedom in relationships. It is impossible to jump to a vMeme we think we would prefer. The baby is in **Beige**, the toddler in **Purple**, bonding to its family. The two-year old reaches **Red** and demands to be heard. School years pass mostly in **Blue**, then we have to take responsibility for our lives and make a living in **Orange** before we are ready for **Green**. Every spiritual teacher is badgered by penniless young hopefuls longing for **Green**, but far from ready as they have not yet taken charge of their own lives in **Orange**. When circumstances deprive an individual of a healthy experience of a vMeme, he or she compensates. For example, an unloved child, lacking **Purple** family bonding and loyalty, may seek these in a **Red** street gang.

6 A 'meme stack' is a cross-section of a human spiral, showing a profile of the relative strength of each layer nested in the stack. We think about many different things, so may well think in different ways in various areas of our lives. Participating in competitive sport activates our **Red**, meditating our **Green**, a family celebration our **Purple**. Observing the emergence of these vMemes in oneself and others is a good way to absorb these concepts, always remembering that vMemes are *not* personality types.

7 vMemes cluster in groups of six.
Beige, **Purple**, **Red**, **Blue**, **Orange** and **Green**
constitute the First Tier, where no-one can fully
understand or appreciate the other world-views. The
Second Tier, beginning with **Yellow**, constitutes a
transformation, a genuine quantum leap, a momentous
jump in consciousness.

Observe carefully if someone claims to have reached
Second Tier. They may understand it intellectually and
believe they reached it, but are they *living* it?

SDi demonstrates clearly how consciousness unfolds
and realises itself, embracing what came before,
transcending and including it. The psychological
evidence for the existence of these stages in human
minds is overwhelming.

For the philosophers and academics among you, **Beige**
corresponds to Archaic Consciousness, **Purple** to
Tribal, **Red** to Warrior, **Blue** to Traditional, **Orange** to
modernist, **Green** to post-modern, and **Yellow** to
Integral consciousness.

As Ken Wilber says, for the first time we can vividly
grasp the entire spectrum of development and
understand that each wave is crucially important for the
health of the overall Spiral.

In 1974, Professor Graves foresaw three possibilities:

-   a massive regression to **Beige** and **Purple** if we fail
to stabilise our weapons and endangered resources.

-   a version of Orwell's *1984,* embodied in **Blue**/**Orange**/**Green** tyrannical, manipulative government with glossed over communitarian overtones.

-   the emergence of a Second Tier approach to business and society, equipped to act locally and plan globally while acting globally and planning locally at the same time.

We are the first generation *taking conscious control* of human evolution. The choice is ours.

CHAPTER 4 - CHANGE

Nothing is permanent but change - Heraclitus

The whole world seems to be clamouring for change. But change *from* what *to* what? by whom? for whom? and how?

For each of us the answer is different. Many think they would be happy if others would change. But we cannot change others, we can only change ourselves. So if we want to improve a relationship - with family, neighbours, business, the world - the best option is to examine our own perceptions and beliefs first.

We all have opinions that we argue strongly for, or against, or choose to remain indifferent to. And never stop to think where we got those ideas. Why should we? They are *ours* so they must be right! All decent people think the same way!

Yet nearly all our opinions are inculcated by parents, school, peer group, employers, friends, newspapers, TV, books. We then defend those ideas vigorously - or fight them because we dislike or distrust those people or organisations.

Why does most of *our* group think the same way? Because the environment we live in has shaped our thinking. Our vMemetic musical chord may be playing a different or similar tune to others. The dissonance repels. The harmony attracts.

Fundamentally, SDi is about change and how to manage it. We will expand on this in a future volume. Meanwhile this chapter has space only for a brief introduction, offered with the hope that it will encourage readers to focus more intently when they think or talk about change.

There are eight variations of change, spread between Horizontal, Oblique and Vertical Change.

HORIZONTAL CHANGE

These are adjustments *within* an unchanged vMeme:

1 - Fine tuning the system without changing the world-view: making minor changes to attitudes, ideas and beliefs. Would a new logo attract attention and improve the business? Could a new dress or a candle-lit dinner revive a fading romantic relationship?

2 - Again without changing the world-view, re-structuring the business and reviewing its ideas and attitudes. Is that fading relationship worth reviving? The same political party stays in power, but a cabinet reshuffle may bring in fresh ideas.

3 – An expansion of thinking could mean a new version of an older process or product, e.g. organic baked beans, automatic machinery to make the same product.

Serial marriages and serial business failures show when lessons have not been learned and barriers to understanding have not been dismantled.

4 - Dropping back to an earlier system temporarily to cope with an internal or external crisis. When under pressure, we tend to revert to what was once familiar and trusted, though it may not be what is required now.

5 - Stretching the existing system to achieve a specific temporary objective. This may be stressful, but often carries the seed of what it is possible to achieve.

OBLIQUE CHANGE

This means adding *selected elements* of more complex thinking. It often reverts to habit when stressed, but if the foundations are strong it may result in a surge towards a new worldview.

6 - Removing blockages and barriers, and abandoning rigid positions, represents revolutionary change. Faced with a crisis, people in healthy vMemes will make decisions and take previously unthinkable action to avert a looming catastrophe such as divorce or bankruptcy.

VERTICAL CHANGE

This is awakening to the *next level* of thinking. It builds on the merits of all earlier stages, but conditions have changed so much and the conceptual space expanded so far that you cannot move back again.

7 - The old order is subsumed into the new system. Often sparked by technological advances that seem

frightening at first. **Purple/Red tribal anarchy** yields to **Blue law and order. Orange competitiveness and greed** open to **Green understanding of the interconnectedness of all life.**

8 - Quantum change shifts a civilisation to a new era. From the Bronze Age to the Iron Age, the agricultural, industrial and information age revolutions.

With the world around us apparently in turmoil, it is fascinating to observe what is going on through SDi lenses. To watch old orders crumbling, the desperation fuelling tribal wars, the disclosure of things that those in power want to keep hidden, and to sense the new incoming energies that can, if we are willing, expand the consciousness of enough people to Second Tier to guide and lead the rest of us into a better future.

<u>CONDITIONS FOR CHANGE</u>

There are six crucial conditions for VERTICAL vMEME CHANGE to take place.

1.The POTENTIAL for more complex thinking in the individual or collective mind/brain. This can be:

> OPEN - The healthiest form with the most possibilities for adjustment, able to change thinking and move freely as life conditions require. Deals effectively with barriers to further development.

> ARRESTED - Trapped within the self or the situation, as barriers have not been overcome.

These may be commitments to care, a lack of insight, or making excuses to disguise fear. Or rationalising the status quo: 'mustn't rock the boat,' 'that's the way things are,' 'one of these days.' Until there is more dissonance or discomfort in the situation, there will be no effort to change.

CLOSED - May lack the neurological or brain power, or has closed down as a result of past trauma. Is insatiable for guarantees of love, cares for only a handful of people, and does not even recognise barriers. Feels threatened by change and over-reacts to the prospect. Anyone thinking differently is a fool. Fights to maintain the status quo.

2. SOLUTIONS - Must be found to current inner or outer problems or threats at the present level. (This can be change within a stage as well).

3. DISSONANCE - Between present thinking and current reality, i.e. it becomes obvious that something is not quite right and that more of the same no longer works.

4. BARRIERS to change (external and internal) must be identified and dealt with fully, not denied, brushed under the carpet, or blamed on someone else.

5. INSIGHT into probable causes and viable alternatives. Until we understand why things went

wrong, lasting change is illusory. It is essential to consider different plans and precisely how they can be implemented.

6. CONSOLIDATION and SUPPORT. Significant change inevitably brings confusion at first, with steep learning curves, false starts and misunderstanding, not to say punishment, from those who do not grasp what is happening and who feel threatened or left out. Support is needed to shore up changes and prevent backsliding until transition to the new vMeme is securely consolidated.

One way of looking at this process, taken from the Ageless Wisdom teachings, is that our Souls engineer crises to confront us so that we learn and understand what we need to push us out of a situation that we have mastered - and where we are therefore comfortable - into a new way of living on a higher level.

Our consciousness is expanded during the struggle between worn-out ideas and new ones, between more of the same that no longer works and entirely new solutions. New energy flows through us opening doorways of opportunity where we least expect them, and we realise that unconsciously we have been preparing for them for years.

In the next chapter we will look at some more aspects of change - specifically how to recognise what is happening in our own lives and all around us.

<u>First Tier reactions to a major crisis that blocks emergence:</u>

BEIGE — **curls up and doesn't want to know**

PURPLE — **retreats into fear and superstition, or runs home to Mummy**

RED — **blames everyone else and fights its corner**

BLUE — **looks for the guilty party, organising witch-hunts and crusades**

ORANGE — **does shady deals if that is what it takes to win**

GREEN — **assumes holier than thou attitude of political correctness**

<u>Second Tier reactions are usually healthy but become unhealthy when it sees what to do but withdraws and does not act:</u>

YELLOW — **evaluates the situation and goes or stays**

TURQUOISE — **looks for the deeper meaning and global impact**

CHAPTER 5 - TRANSCEND and INCLUDE

In Chapter 4 we saw that before we can grow into a new psychological space, various conditions have to be met. This sounds daunting, yet we have all done this several times since we were babies!

Looking back over your own life to identify the stages you have lived through helps you to recognise where others are now. Recalling your own experience – how did you think, feel, act in those days? What did you hope for? What did you fear? What did you believe in? Then even if you are in dispute with others, you can relate to them in a non-threatening, helpful, understanding way. In other words speak according to their level of consciousness, just as you do when speaking to a child.

As our consciousness expands, our brains evolve to handle increasing complexity. Growing into a new vMeme involves *transcending and including* the previous ones.

The need to satisfy basic **Beige** physiological needs continues all our lives. As does the healthy **Purple** need for bonding, the healthy **Red** need to have fun, be creative and free enough to explore and enjoy life, and healthy **Blue** peace of mind and hope for the future.

During the entering stage of a new vMeme (we will explore this in detail in the next volume) we carry much of the previous one with us. Gradually, we let go of the habits and relationships that are no longer appropriate. This may be painful, and we may be lonely for a while before we are integrated into our new life conditions. Family and old friends may not understand and feel hurt, and it takes time to make new friends and adjust to the thinking, behaviour, work, books, music and even diet of our new life-style.

Years later, when we have completed the experience, learned the lessons and found solutions to problems in this new vMeme, we begin to react against it. Chafing against authoritarian **Blue,** disliking the competitiveness and failure to care for people in **Orange**, or doubting the effectiveness of **Green** collectivism and consensus decision-making. We are preparing to move on again.

vMemes develop like waves approaching a beach, we see only the nearest, which conceals the one behind. It is only when the nearest reaches its peak and begins to disintegrate that the one behind it rises to take its place and becomes visible. In the same way, in individuals, societies and civilisations, the new is growing within, often unconsciously, until it suddenly breaks through and life is permanently changed.

However if we have resisted change, by ignoring or failing to deal with current problems - or by putting up with things 'to avoid rocking the boat' - we may well experience an accident, or illness, or what to us is a disaster. This plunges us into a 'gamma trap' where we feel angry and powerless and are eventually forced to face reality and understand what went wrong and why.

But where the six conditions for change have largely been met, we can take charge of our lives and act before disaster strikes.

Change happens in the same way for individuals, groups, societies and whole civilisations. Many people are frightened by current economic, political and environmental changes in the world and the crumbling of old structures that we thought we could rely on.

History shows that in times of greatest human crisis, great Teachers have appeared - Sri Krishna, Lao-tsu, Buddha, Socrates, Christ, Mahomet – inspiring the creation of civilisations of greater enlightenment, founding new religions, and still influencing us today. Many lesser known avatars have also walked among us, bringing new energies that stimulated our spiritual growth – all part of a continuing process of revelation.

The concept of a spiritual hierarchy is fundamental to most belief systems. Man has universally believed that beings of greater power, wisdom, knowledge and ability exist on some higher level than our own and watch over the inhabitants of Earth. The spiritual impulse within us, the yearning and striving towards some greater good is part of our make-up as human beings – and is expressed according to our life conditions.

Those of us in the 'first world' have come a long way since **Purple** and **Red** days when we feared and placated terrifying and wilful gods. The current great religions emerged during the thousand years known as the Axial Age, sweeping humanity away from tribal life and towards the development of individual consciousness.

Jesus taught that we each have a soul and are loved by God, and the value of service – thereby providing *meaning and purpose* for our lives and laying the foundations of moral responsibility. We were into **Blue**. Whether we go to church or not, and whether or not we are aware of the deeper mystic aspects of our religion, these teachings are alive within us: the knowledge of right and wrong, our sense of responsibility, the need to care for others and the aspiration to be good.

Eventually the dogmatism of the church threatened to stifle the development of independent thought, and this led to another explosion of consciousness – the Enlightenment, igniting the scientific revolution that defines our modern world. We were into **Orange**, self-conscious and claiming autonomy. We ignored or arrogantly dismissed the concept of a God, Source or Creator. Atheists poured scorn on caricatures of God, and our in-built spiritual aspiration was perverted to self-interest and the worship of false gods: money, celebrity, 'progress' and technological marvels. Science had become the new belief system.

Dissatisfaction with **Orange** led us into **Green** which reawakened our spirituality, and our understanding has been increased immeasurably by the exchange of Eastern and Western thought. Our current crisis is huge, so should we be looking for a new great Teacher – for the reappearance of the Christ on earth to save us? Apart from the practicalities of how He would appear – on TV? wearing modern clothes? - the idea of being saved is very appealing. But we must cease to personalise the Christ consciousness. We are no longer children waiting for a loving parent to kiss us better and sort out our problems. We are entering Yellow - becoming *conscious that we are conscious.* And therefore responsible for ourselves. Responsible for our own evolution. Actively cooperating with the great creative principle that gave birth to us and the entire manifest world.

A major task now is to make a conscious choice to follow some psychological or spiritual discipline that will enable us to achieve personal mastery and develop the qualities of love, compassion, goodwill and empathy. A first step might be to shift our thinking from negative to positive. Counting the number of times in a day you hear negativity expressed, or do so yourself, will shock you. It has become a form of protection against the fears and desires of the personal self that arise in their particular life conditions.

And one of these fears is what will happen when we die. There is plenty of evidence that consciousness continues, but we find it very difficult indeed to conceive what that might mean without a body attached.

The positive answer is to align ourselves more and more with higher consciousness – or thinking and acting as if we are already soul-infused - until the world of fear and desire falls away. It is rather like setting off in a hot-air balloon – you feel no movement as the ground drops away below you.

There is only one consciousness, of which we are all a part subjectively, whether we are aware of it or not. According to Carl Jung, humanity is united in the collective unconscious.

Consciously, we are connecting through a global electronic network – which in itself does not unify our consciousness – but it is the means by which the vision of unification of the consciousness of humanity can be spread.

I believe that many highly evolved beings are here working among us already, in every field of endeavour, preparing our minds and hearts for the great awakening that is already in progress.

CHAPTER 6 - WHERE ARE WE NOW?

'All that is necessary for evil to triumph is for good men and women to do nothing.'
Edmund Burke.

Many of us are discouraged by global problems: climate, population, poverty, the extinction of species, terrorism, dwindling resources, changes in the balance of economic power, and turmoil everywhere we look. Or daunted by the moral choices posed by advances in science and technology - eg. genetic engineering. Others just don't want to know - they have enough personal worries, thank you. Hence the widespread retreat into cynicism, nostalgia, escapism and virtual living online. It is not easy now to perceive the essential divinity in all human beings.

Professor Clare Graves, originator of the research and the theory now known as Spiral Dynamics Integral, predicted a 'momentous leap' for humankind. Dr. Don Beck says that we should not be discouraged by economic and political collapse, as before major change, society *regresses* to old methods and values.

One step backwards to prepare for the leap forward: a leap into the Second Tier, and Yellow and Turquoise consciousness from which we will have an overview of and empathy with all fellow human beings, and the ability to solve old problems with new more complex thinking.

People in many countries are trying to break free from their current Life Conditions in a three-pronged movement across the globe.

1. Billions in **Purple** and **Red** are trying to escape poverty, repression and various forms of social and psychological feudalism - and find meaning and purpose in **Blue**.
2. Others are trying to escape the *isms* of **Blue** and enjoy individual freedom and the good life in **Orange**.
3. **Green**, fuelled by guilt and too much materialism, is determined to attack any form of injustice that rewards one 'class' of humans over another.
For all these people, these are huge steps forward in evolution.

Around the world aggressive tribal communities are evolving from **Purple** into **Red**. This is not new. Countless others - including our own ancestors - have done so, waging bloody battles until they get tired of fighting and welcome the rudiments of **Blue** law and order.

The problem now is that they are armed not with spears and swords, but with Kalashnikovs and bombs. So instead of seeing these as local problems that can safely be left to sort themselves out as the consciousness of the participants grows, we move in with our big guns, and cameras, to 'free' them and 'give' them democracy. But until they have experienced **Blue** discipline and thereby learned *self*-discipline, they interpret our efforts according to their own thinking, which is **Purple** and **Red**.

Closer to home our 'feral youth' are living in the same vMemes. They may never have bonded in **Purple** with their families, and compensate by bonding with a gang. None of them have experienced discipline and have not learned self-discipline, so their thinking is **Red** - ready to turn everything we say or do to their own advantage. The **Blue** structures in society that coped with wild youth over the centuries have been steadily dismantled over the past fifty years, and need to be rebuilt in new ways, because the healthy functioning of all the Memes - including **Blue** - is essential to the overall health and strength of the spiral.

The Middle East is a bubbling cauldron of tribes and other **Purple** residues of the break-up of the Ottoman Empire still percolating under the sand; the impact of **Orange** Western imperialistic ventures; fiercely competing **Red** /**Blue** religious zealots striving to protect 'their' respective holy places, and the enticement of windfall oil money. Much of the region is still - as far as potential for change is concerned - Closed or Arrested.

Closed-minded True Believers who insist on their -ism - or else! - are not the only reason for the region's difficulties. Behind these are First-World **Orange** versus Second World **Blue** and even Third World **Red** and **Purple**. The world's finest negotiators and conflict management teams have been working there for years. When they have peak **Orange** or **Green** world views, they often make things worse instead of better. And negotiators are often perceived as backing or blaming one side or the other. Like teaching or leadership, arbitration has to function within a half-step or so of the base vMemes.

TERRORISM

Let us take a closer look at one of our big worries, and the shadow side of the vMemes described in previous chapters. Most terrorist behaviour arises from frustration, the need to attack and overcome barriers, or retrieve something lost. It appears when people are confused by chaotic change and transformation, or feel they are being left behind. *Why* people do things much more important than what they do.

The minds behind terrorist acts (the sponsors or beneficiaries) are usually at a higher level of complexity than the actual perpetrators - seeking political advantage (Orange) by exploiting individuals who believe they are fighting evil forces (Blue) or settling ancient scores (Red).

PURPLE - Tribal Terrorism Assaults and purges to preserve tribal honour and sacred ways, honour ancestors, and to kill rivals for food or territory. Examples: ethnic conflicts in Bosnia, Ruanda, Liberia, Idi Amin's Uganda. Inner city ethnic and gang wars. Racial prejudice. Massacres of indigenous peoples. Cult members obedient to a god figure. Killing a daughter in love with a 'wrong' man to preserve family honour.
Personality type: obedience to chiefs - belief in signs and omens - anger covering underlying fear - identification with group or clan - willing self-sacrifice for leader's desires.

RED - *Predatory Terrorism* Personal grudges, vendettas, destroy enemies and enhance power. Glorious martyrdom for a cause - kill or be killed - live long in legend if not in fact. Examples: Pol Pot - Mao's Red Brigades - Mugabe - West Bank 'incidents' - war crimes - native American scalping raids - religious based fanatical religious militants.

Personality type: seeks personal glory and heroic reputation, or revenge. Saves face at all costs - no feelings of guilt - no regard for the consequences - does not value human life.

BLUE - *Dogmatic Terrorism* Fights against evil in the name of a political system, religion, or other all-powerful 'Truth.' Righteous defence and extension of the one True Way as agents of Divine will - cleansing evil and smiting evildoers. Examples: the holocaust, Yugoslavia, Chechnya - absolutist religious fundamental theocrats such as Jihadin - the Inquisition - skinheads - KKK - IRA Contras.

Personality type : needs law, order and stability - racist, separatist, blind faith, fights "wrong" authority to the death - disciplined, duty bound - willing to sacrifice self for reward to come.

ORANGE - Strategic Terrorism Seeks political and economic advantage through the media, business and finance, using the system against itself. Examples: state sponsored terrorism - arms trafficking - sophisticated military hackers – business reprisals by drug syndicates - attacks on newspapers - economic terrorism.

Personality type: air of superiority - desires recognition.

Buys allegiance and political influence - formulates principles to fit desires, i.e. rationalises - is excited by the game and ruthless when frustrated.

These are the people manipulating us now, through the media, keeping us in fear so that we continue to toe the line - 'hang on to nurse for fear of something worse' – if terrorism becomes stale news, let's have a pandemic or nuclear proliferation to worry about. . . .

GREEN - Eco/Info-Terrorism Attacks environment, infrastructure and information systems to stop exploitation and free the human spirit. Claim to act on behalf of living things and oppose crimes against humanity, liberate the oppressed and prevent waste and needless consumption. Examples: animal rights activists - 'peace' attacks on military installations - hacking into computer systems.
Personality type: Smug - self-satisfied.

ALL the above need help to evolve. *That* is what we have to address. The disastrous phrase 'war on terrorism' just puts up defensive barriers and provides more justification for their actions.

MOVING INTO SECOND TIER YELLOW

When our consciousness is locked into one of the first tier vMemes above, we cannot possibly see the whole picture, though we think we do!

Einstein memorably said that we cannot solve problems with the thinking that caused the problems. So it is essential for us to change our thinking, shift the focus, see the whole situation from a wider viewpoint, with a fresh set of assumptions abut human nature. In other words, make the tremendous leap into **YELLOW** and Second Tier consciousness.

What can you do as an individual to achieve this? See the six crucial conditions for Meme change in Chapter 4: have the potential, solve problems at present level, realise that more of the same no longer works, identify and deal with barriers to change, have insight into the cause of problems and consider possible plans in detail, and find support during the confusing period of shifting into Second Tier.

So what does it look like when we get there? Spiral Dynamics Integral offers a new way of connecting individuals or groups of any kind and any size. It is called Meshworks and will be described in detail in a future volume of the *Emergence* series. Static for strength and permanence. Flow for resilience, flexibility and a morphing capacity. This is a *meshing* not a melting pot - individuals and organisations each contributing the best of what they are without becoming lost in a common blob. Like a traditional jazz band, each player expertly extemporising on the same air, producing a sound much greater than its parts.

To move forward together into a higher level of existence for everyone here on earth, we have to change two ingrained habits:
1. Our piecemeal, ad hoc, fragmented, competitive approach to problem resolution.

2. The way these complex problems are overlaid with racial and ethnic poison, compromising every initiative and polarising the elements which should be working in concert with each other.

SDi reveals the hierarchies of complexity beneath the surface of our society, enabling us to focus our efforts on the huge gaps and imbalances that plague social order round the world, pay attention to different world views and diverse realities, collaborate on all initiatives in public and private sectors and weave them together in a spiral-like coil where everything connects to everything else. If that sounds impossible, it shows how heavily the shackles of past thinking lie upon us!

The urge to achieve a higher state of being has impelled human beings through all the ages, and we stand on the shoulders of all the seekers that have gone before us, ready to cooperate in the prodigious task of emergence: raising the consciousness of the human race and making space for the lower kingdoms to evolve.

*The fragmentary consciousness of the human frame is
seeing its way towards the Soul, the Self,
the Whole from which it came, and is set, like an
aircraft turning on to the take-off runway, to begin the
flight which will lift it into the sun.*
Michal Eastcott

**Watch out for *Emergence Vol 2 –
Climb the Spiral***

This will explore for each vMeme the entering phase of
preparation and excitement; the peak phase of
apparent stability (which we saw in Chapter 2 above);
and an exiting period of disintegration as problems
outstrip the capacity to deal with them.

GLOSSARY

vMEME - vMEME reflects a world view, a valuing system, a level of psychological existence, a belief structure, an organising principle, a way of thinking or a mode of adjustment. It represents, firstly then, a core intelligence that forms systems and directs human behaviour. Secondly, it impacts upon all life choices as a decision making framework. Thirdly, each vMEME can manifest itself in both healthy and unhealthy forms. Fourthly, such a vMEME is a discrete structure for thinking, not just a set of ideas, values or cause. Fifthly, it can brighten and dim as the Life Conditions (consisting of historic Times, geographic Place, existential Problems, and societal Circumstances) change.

USEFUL RESOURCES

CDs

Spiral Dynamics Integral by Don Beck, PhD. (Sounds True Learning Course, 6 CDs)
The most comprehensive source. ISBN 1-59179-425-0.

BOOKS

Spiral Dynamics, Mastering Values, Leadership and Change by Don Edward Beck and Christopher C. Cowan (Blackwell 1996) The classic text book on SDi.

Integral Consciousness and the Future of Evolution by Steve McIntosh. (Paragon House 2007) An excellent overview of the development of integral thought.

The Reflexive Universe by Arthur M Young (Anodos 1976) Demonstrates that the entire universe is a purpose driven *process* that proceeds in stages, each transcending and including previous stages.

A Brief History of Everything by Ken Wilber (1996)

A Theory of Everything by Ken Wilber (2001)

'I' The Story of the Self by Michal Eastcott (Sundial House 1980) Lots of insights for those seeking a meaning to life.

Heart Awakening – Your Path to Unconditional Love and Healing by Raoult Bertrand (1997/2008)

MAGAZINES

Kosmos - an integral approach to global awakening. Leading edge thinking and beautiful artwork.
www.kosmosjournal.org

WEBSITES

www.humanemergence.org
www.spiraldynamics.net
www.creativegroupmeditation.org
www.rosemarywilkie.co.uk
www.lucistrust.org

RESEARCH AND DIAGNOSTIC TOOLS

An extensive array of assessments and surveys are available through Christopher Cooke who may be contacted at Christopher.cookee@5deep.net or www.5deep.net or www.3lm.network

TRAINING AND ADVISORY SERVICES IN HUMAN EMERGENCE

The Sundial House Group & The International Group for Creative Meditation offer mentored training based on the work of Roberto Assagioli, the founder of Psychosynthesis and a pioneer in promoting the expansion of consciousness.
www.creativegroupmeditation.org

A full spectrum accredited training and advisory service using what is known as the Human Emergence Framework is offered through www.5deep.net or www.3lm.network

Printed in Great Britain
by Amazon